Ancient Roman
TECHNOLOGY

Amelie von Zumbusch

For my father

Published in 2014 by The Rosen Publishing Group, Inc.
29 East 21st Street, New York, NY 10010

First Edition

Book Design: Kate Vlachos
Layout Design: Andrew Povolny

Photo Credits: Cover Marco Maccarini/E+/Getty Images; p. 4 DEA/L. Pedicini/De Agostini/Getty Images; p. 5 iStockphoto/Thinkstock; p. 6 Dan Porges/Photo Library/ Getty Images; p. 7 (top) Alberto Pizzoli/AFP/Getty Images; p. 7 (bottom) Martin Child/ Digital Vision/Getty Images; p. 9 Ian Murray/age fotostock/Getty Images; p. 10 edo/Shutterstock.com; p. 11 JMN/Cover/Getty Images; p. 12 Vincenzo Lombardo/ Photographers's Choice/Getty Images; p. 13 Hemera/Thinkstock; p. 14 Werner Forman/ Universal Images Group/Getty Images; p. 15 DEA/A. Dagli Orti/De Agostini Picture Library/Getty Images; p. 16 Universal Images Group/Getty Images; p. 17, 19 DEA Picture Library/Getty Images; p. 20 Roman/The Bridgeman Art Library/Getty Images; p. 21 Samuel Magal/Sites & Photos/Getty Images; p. 22 Photos.com/Thinkstock.

Library of Congress Cataloging-in-Publication Data

Zumbusch, Amelie von.
 Ancient Roman technology / by Amelie von Zumbusch. — First edition.
    pages cm. — (Spotlight on ancient civilizations: Rome)
Includes index.
 ISBN 978-1-4777-0780-7 (library binding) — ISBN 978-1-4777-0893-4 (pbk.) — ISBN 978-1-4777-0894-1 (6-pack)
 1. Technology—Rome—History—Juvenile literature. 2. Rome—Civilization—Juvenile literature. I. Title.
 T16.Z86 2014
 609.37—dc23
                                      2013004135

Manufactured in the United States of America

CPSIA Compliance Information: Batch #S13PK2: For Further Information contact Rosen Publishing, New York, New York at 1-800-237-9932

CONTENTS

Ancient Roman Technology

One of the things about ancient Roman **civilization** that most impresses people today is the Romans' use of **technology**. Technology covers both how people use tools to do things and the tools that they use. Big building projects were some of the main things that the Romans used technology for.

This is a model of a Roman noria. A noria is a tool that is used to raise water from a stream. Norias were generally used to water crops.

One famous building that was built with Roman concrete is the Colosseum. This arena in Rome was used for sports events and entertainment.

The Romans discovered a new kind of concrete. They used it in many of their big projects. To make it, they mixed water and quicklime. They made quicklime by baking the rock limestone. Then they mixed in ash from volcanoes. The Romans often mixed stones and bricks into their concrete for added strength.

Arches, Vaults, and Domes

Some of the most important construction methods that the Romans used in their building projects were arches, vaults, and domes. An arch is a curved span that covers an opening. Arches support weight better than flat-topped openings. The Romans often placed arches side-by-side to form arcades.

Though arches are good at carrying weight, they need to be supported on each side.

This room is in the House of Augustus, on Rome's Palatine Hill. It uses a barrel vault for the ceiling.

A vault is a ceiling that is built using arch technology. Barrel vaults look like arches that are stretched out long. When two barrel vaults cross, they form a groin vault.

Domes are rounded vaults. The Romans were the first people to build really big domes. These domes provided the world's first big, open, indoor spaces.

The biggest Roman dome is in the Pantheon. At its base, the dome is 142 feet (43 m) wide. It is the same height, as measured from the floor.

Heating Technology

The Romans developed impressive heating technology for buildings. Air was heated in a furnace, generally by burning wood. The air flowed through a space under the floor, called a **hypocaust**. This warmed rooms. Concrete and tile pillars supported the floor above the hypocaust. Tiles with hollow centers in the walls created **flues**. Heated air escaped through these. They helped warm rooms, too.

The hypocaust system was the world's first central heating system. The Romans used it to heat public baths. They also used it in homes in provinces where the weather got chillier than it did in Rome. Provinces were lands that the Romans had **conquered**.

These are the remains of a hypocaust that the Romans built in Great Britain. You can see the pillars that held up the floor.

9

Bringing Water to Cities

The Romans used a system of channels, called aqueducts, to bring clean water to Rome and other cities. Water flows downhill. Therefore, aqueducts sloped slightly downward.

Arcade bridges let aqueducts cross valleys without blocking them. They also saved money because they used less building material than a solid wall would have.

The Romans sometimes built dams to collect water for aqueducts. One example is the Proserpina Dam, near Mérida, Spain. This dam is still in use today!

Aqueducts carried water long distances. Much of the time, water flowed through underground trenches. Tunnels carried it under hills. Walls carried it over dips in the landscape. Arcade bridges spanned bigger valleys. Pipe systems that relied on water pressure were also used in valleys.

The water from aqueducts pooled in basins outside cities. From there, it flowed into cities through pipes. It fed into public fountains, toilets, and baths. Only the rich had water in their own homes.

Roads and Bridges

The Romans built a road network across the lands they ruled. The military built the main highways. Good roads let soldiers get places quickly. This helped them stay in control.

One of the best-known Roman highways is the Appian Way. It was eventually lengthened to run from Rome to Brindisi, in southeastern Italy.

The Romans often built single-arch bridges when a road needed to cross a small stream like this one.

Military **surveyors** studied the landscape and planned road routes. Soldiers cleared the routes. They cut down trees, moved rocks, and dug trenches in which to build roads. They filled the trenches with several layers of sand, gravel, and stones. The top layer was either packed gravel or cut paving stones.

In marshy areas, roads sometimes rested on wood platforms. Arcade bridges crossed river valleys and other uneven ground. Simple bridges crossed smaller streams.

Many Metals

Early on, the Romans **imported** metal. Later, they set up mines in Spain, Great Britain, and other provinces. The Romans dug **shafts** to let heat and bad air escape mines. Waterwheels drained water from some mines. However, mining was still dangerous work.

Smiths processed **ore** from the mines. They shaped the resulting metal into useful things. Copper, silver, and gold were used for coins and jewelry. Copper and tin were mixed to make bronze for weapons and tools. Iron was used for tools and weapons, too. The Romans used lead for many things, including makeup, dishes, and water pipes.

The image on this Roman coin honors a Roman military victory. This coin is a silver *denarius*.

This Roman carving shows a goldsmith at work. Some of the richest Roman gold mines were in northwestern Spain, southern Wales, and what is now Austria.

Military Technology

During Rome's long history, its military and military technology changed. Early on, **citizens** were called on to fight in times of war. They supplied their own weapons. Later, the Romans set up the world's first professional military. Its well organized units were called legions. Auxiliary troops of non-Romans sometimes fought alongside the legions.

This carving shows a soldier from a Roman legion. The size of legions changed over time. They could have as many as 6,000 soldiers each.

16

By the third century BC, the main weapon soldiers used was a short sword, called a *gladius*. They also carried a *pugio*, or dagger, and long spears for throwing, called *pila*. Some troops also carried a long spear, called a *hasta*. A soldier's helmet, armor, and shield, called a *scutum*, provided protection.

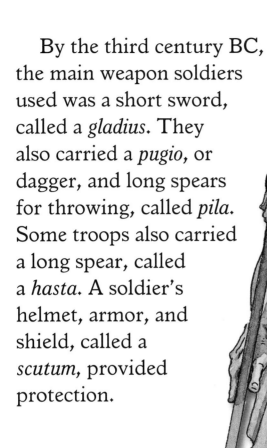

Some auxiliary soldiers, such as the one in this modern drawing, used Roman weapons. Others used the traditional weapons of their people.

Roman Ships

Though Rome is near the Mediterranean Sea, the early Romans did not have a navy. That changed when Rome went to war against Carthage in 264 BC. Carthage had a powerful navy. The Romans captured a Carthaginian warship. They made copies and added hinged bridges for boarding enemy ships. The Romans won the war!

Roman warships were galleys, or oar-powered ships. Trading ships were often galleys, too. Some galleys used square sails when the wind was right. Triangular sails appeared around the second century AD. These are called lateen sails because the sailors who first used them spoke the Romans' language, Latin!

The front ship in this Roman mosaic is a galley. A mosaic is a picture made of tiny pieces of tile or stone.

Medicine and Public Health

The Romans did not know as much about medicine as we do today. For example, dried hyena skin was said to cure people who had been bitten by mad dogs! Doctors were skilled at **surgery**, though. The Romans got much of their medical knowledge from the Greeks. Roman doctors often came from Greece. Many were **slaves** or former slaves.

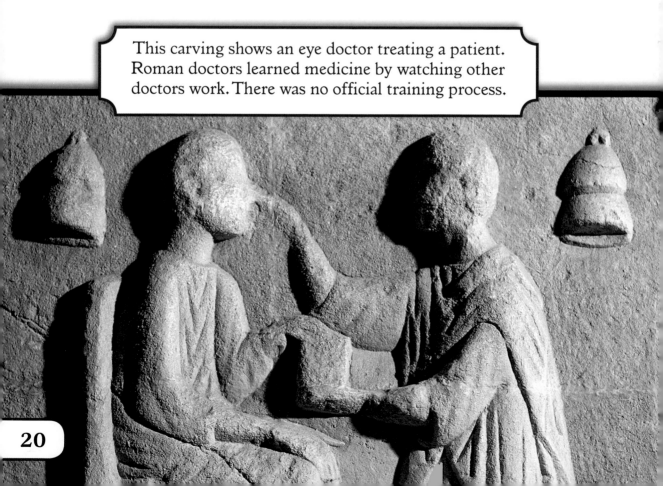

This carving shows an eye doctor treating a patient. Roman doctors learned medicine by watching other doctors work. There was no official training process.

These are the remains of the toilets at the Baths of the Cyclops in Dougga, Tunisia. The town is known for its well-preserved Roman ruins.

Roman cities were very clean for their time. This limited the spread of sickness. The Romans visited public baths often. Aqueducts provided clean drinking water. They also supplied a constant flow of water that kept public toilets clean. Sewers carried away waste and wastewater.

Still Shaping Our World

The early Romans used a complicated calendar. In 46 BC, Roman leader Julius Caesar asked **astronomers** to develop a better one. This new calendar had 365 days, with a leap year every fourth February. The calendar we use today is based on it.

Roman astronomers were not always right. We now know that Earth circles the Sun, not the other way around. However, we still name the planets in our solar system after Roman gods. The Romans continue to shape our world!

In 44 BC, the month of July was renamed in honor of Julius Caesar. The English name for the month comes from his name, too.

GLOSSARY

astronomers (uh-STRAH-nuh-merz) People who study the Sun, the Moon, the planets, and the stars.

citizens (SIH-tih-zenz) People who live in a country or other community and have certain rights.

civilization (sih-vih-lih-ZAY-shun) People living in a certain way.

conquered (KON-kerd) Overcame something.

flues (FLOOZ) Tubes through which smoke and other gases can escape.

imported (im-POR-ted) Brought from another country for sale or use.

hypocaust (HY-puh-kawst) A space under a floor that is heated by gases from a fire or furnace.

ore (OR) Rock that contains metal.

shafts (SHAFTZ) Long, thin stems or openings.

slaves (SLAYVZ) People who are "owned" by other people and forced to work for them.

surgery (SER-juh-ree) An operation.

surveyors (ser-VAY-erz) People who measure land.

technology (tek-NAH-luh-jee) The way that people do something using tools and the tools that they use.

INDEX

WEBSITES

Due to the changing nature of Internet links, PowerKids Press has developed an online list of websites related to the subject of this book. This site is updated regularly. Please use this link to access the list:
www.powerkidslinks.com/sacr/tech/